D0305328

Fun and flirty secrets for

_____

From your fabulous friend

_____

THE

Decadent

HOUSEWIFE

THE Decadent HOUSEWIFE

FUN AND FLIRTY SECRETS TO KEEP HIM WRAPPED AROUND YOUR LITTLE FINGER

ROSEMARY COUNTER

Reader's Digest

The Reader's Digest Association, Inc.
New York, NY/Montreal

A READER'S DIGEST BOOK

Copyright © 2011 Elwin Street Limited

Conceived and produced by
Elwin Street Limited
144 Liverpool Road
London N1 1LA
www.elwinstreet.com

All rights reserved. Unauthorized reproduction, in any manner, is prohibited.

Reader's Digest is a registered trademark of The Reader's Digest Association, Inc.

FOR READER'S DIGEST
U.S. Project Editor: Kim Casey
Senior Art Director: George McKeon
Executive Editor, Trade Publishing: Dolores York
Associate Publisher, Trade Publishing: Rosanne McManus
President and Publisher, Trade Publishing: Harold Clarke

Library of Congress Cataloging in Publication Data
Counter, Rosemary.
 The decadent housewife : fun and flirty secrets to keep him wrapped around your little finger /
Rosemary Counter.
     p. cm.
 Includes index.
 ISBN 978-1-60652-252-3
 1. Housewives--Humor. 2. Women--Humor. I. Title.
 PN6231.H74C68 2011
 818'.602--dc22
                        2010041074

Interior design by Ingrid Paulson and Tracy Timson

Photo Credits:
Cover image: Corbis Images.
Advertising Archive: pp. 16,19, 62; Corbis: pp. 51, 77; Dreamstime: pp. 4, 14, 15, 22, 23, 24, 25,
32, 33, 34, 35, 40, 42, 43, 48, 49, 53, 58, 66, 67, 74, 76, 87, 89, 90, 91, 99, 104, 105, 106, 110, 111;
iStockphoto: pp. 10, 11, 12, 13, 21, 30, 31, 33, 37, 38, 39, 41, 42, 43, 46, 48, 49, 52, 56, 59, 64, 66,
67, 70, 73, 78, 79, 82, 83, 85, 88, 89, 92, 96, 97, 98, 99, 104, 105, 108, 100, 101, 112; Time
Tunnel: pp. 8, 28, 36, 44, 60, 68, 80, 84, 94.
Elwin Street Ltd has made every effort to contact copyright holders of the images reproduced in
this book. We will be happy to correct in subsequent editions any errors brought to our attention.

We are committed to both the quality of our products and the service we provide to our
customers. We value your comments, so please feel free to contact us:

        The Reader's Digest Association, Inc.
        Adult Trade Publishing
        44 S. Broadway
        White Plains, NY 10601

For more Reader's Digest products and information, visit our website:
        www.rd.com (in the United States)

Printed in China

1 3 5 7 9 10 8 6 4 2

CONTENTS

Introduction

Sure you're a housewife, but are you a Decadent Housewife?

Every woman, whether she's a corporate lawyer or cocktail waitress, has a moment of awakening. Tired and ungroomed, she finally realizes: What's much more fun than going to work? *Not* going to work. But what would she do all day? Whatever she feels like doing. But what about the Women's Movement? She now has plenty of time to read *The Second Shift* in the bath. And what's more girl power than sending a man out to do it for you? Nothing.

This is not to say you don't contribute. In fact, your mere presence is your contribution. You can't cook, of course, but you sure look cute in an apron. Housecleaning disgusts you, obviously, but you know the number of a nice woman who thrives on it. You can't always hold your dirty martinis (they usually get a good hold on you), but you throw an awesome cocktail party.

It therefore goes without saying that *The Decadent Housewife* is not your mother's housekeeping book. (In fact, you should probably never show your mother this book.) Though Mom might know how to cook without setting off the smoke alarm or clean without deliberately getting high on fumes, a Decadent Housewife is a true housekeeper. That's right; it's yours. The house and everything in it—your man, your time, your actual housekeeper—is yours to enjoy.

So start enjoying what's yours today. Whether it's a morning martini or an afternoon art class, *The Decadent Housewife* is your guide to filling your days with fabulousness, feigning the skills as necessary, dressing the part, and micromanaging your man.

But it can be a struggle to fit everything into one day—you are just one woman (albeit a fabulous woman) after all. And, like getting the hang of idleness or the business of party hopping, cultivating the art of Decadent Housewifery is not for the faint of heart (though fainting, you'll learn, is an excellent tactic in your line of work). So to make sure you're making the most of your high-maintenance lifestyle, first spend a day in the life of a real Decadent Housewife.

Whether you need fitness tips for lazy cardiophobes or a much-needed explanation of all those crazy contraptions in your kitchen and what they're actually used for, this is the ultimate guide to finding and nurturing your inner housewife. From leisurely sleeping in to afternoon idleness, it's time to discover the true meaning of decadence. Because you know it's true what they say: It's a hard job, but somebody's got to do it.

Rise and Shine

———

7:30–11:30 A.M.

Good Morning!

Although all Decadent Housewives obviously hate mornings, we know they are crucial to the development and maintenance of the Decadent Housewife lifestyle. Though there is truly nothing worse than being woken by the brazen ring of an alarm, and you are no doubt irritated by your partner's cruel indifference to your sleep preferences, take comfort in the fact that at least you don't have to go to work.

Your man will no doubt be grumpy and somewhat resentful. He is likely exhausted from years of hard work and sleep deprivation. Luckily for you, this has left him in a prime state for your first move of the day.

A Decadent Bonus Tip!
Wear lingerie. It will be far more difficult
for him to stay mad.

The Condition Position

Turn off the alarm and feign a smile. Purr, "Good morning" into his ear, followed with a chosen pet name. "Darling" or "sweetheart" works well for most housewives, but a Decadent Housewife knows to use "stud," "big man," or anything else that reinforces masculinity.

As you gently stroke his ego, whisper, "It's time to go to work," in his ear. This type of stimuli-response training works well on lab rats and your man alike. He will soon learn fond associations and eagerly rise to every occasion. This is also an excellent time for positive reinforcement if you encounter resistance. Emphasize how he is the strongest/smartest/fastest police officer/businessman/ professional baseball player on the force/board/field. If unsure of occupation, use "best man on the team."

Breakfast

Some might say that housewives should always make their men breakfast, but these housewives are simply not decadent. Their efforts grow unappreciated, their toast gets burned, their men complain that today's breakfast wasn't as good as yesterday's. A scrumptious and nutritious breakfast delivered daily is at worst impossible and at best irritating, so it's best that you save your breakfasts for truly special occasions, such as birthdays or apologies for crashing his car.

This is not to say a Decadent Housewife won't benefit from the ghosts of breakfasts past. You can easily tap into fond recollections of that same feeling with the modern breakfast equivalent: coffee. When he is in the shower, turn on the coffeepot. Better yet, invest in a high-tech coffeemaker that will turn itself on so you don't need to get up. Charge this to his Visa card and call it an anniversary present.

Your coffee will definitely not look like this.
That would be ridiculous.

Time it for his morning shower or, if this proves unnecessarily stressful, use this time-out as an excuse to talk to your hot neighbor. He'll likely be thrilled to stop landscaping and give his sweaty bod a break while showcasing his technological skills. Try not to engage in love of the kitchen variety. If this accidentally occurs, make breakfast.

The Decadent Housewife

"BABY, I'M SORRY" PANCAKES

YOU WILL NEED
1 pile flour
1 egg, remove the shell
1 scoop milk, preferably fresh
(If unavailable, consider knocking suggestively
at your hot neighbor's door)

DIRECTIONS
Mix all in mixing bowl. Pour batter on hot buttery pan. When you
smell burning, flip pancake. When you smell it again, you're done.

PRESENTATION
Cover pancake with syrup and/or butter and/or whipped cream
(all available in instant form and with unimportant expiration date).
Add sliced fresh-ish fruit.

"What's a Pancake?"
If this is too hard, consider waffles. They just slide into your new
high-tech toaster investment.

Decadent Bonus Tips!
A pinch of baking powder will make your batter keep
overnight in the fridge.
Consider tricking a more domestically inclined friend into
making it for you. Thank her via martini.

The Sleeping-In Commandments

Oversleeping is a cornerstone of a Decadent Housewife's lifestyle. As soon as you hear the door click shut and his car peel away from the driveway, you know you've successfully scored another day of luxury. If you had to get up to make breakfast/coffee/kiss him good-bye, your next step should be to return to bed—on whichever side you like. Here's how the gods do it.

1. THOU SHALL NOT AWAKEN EARLY...
Getting up before your husband or the sun is both completely unacceptable and contrary to the natural way of the world. It also sets a bad precedent, so don't ruin it for the rest of us.

2. ...NOR TOO LATE
Yes, there is such a thing (just about). An entire day spent in bed might be thought to fall on the side of overly excessive idleness.

3. THOU SHALL LET THY MIND WANDER
This is your chance to ponder life's important questions, such as, "What should I wear today?" Envision your closet from top to bottom packed with all your favorite outfits—and some imaginary additions off the fashion week catwalk. Imagine yourself—a little taller and thinner perhaps—rotating in said ensembles like a mannequin.

4. HAVE SWEET DREAMS!
If your brain wanders to your hunky neighbor, so be it. Now's no time for restraint; fantasies are all fair play.

5. LOUNGE IN STYLE
If it's worth doing, it's worth doing right. And in style. Silky luxury nightwear? Check. Floaty diaphanous dressing gown? Check. Cooling gel eye pack? Check.

The Decadent Housewife

6. THE GUILTY SHALL SUFFER FOR ETERNITY...

No one—not your invasive mother, your jealous husband, the employed—should make you feel bad about your 14-hour sleep therapy (if you call it therapy, maybe they'll leave you alone). It feels good, it is good for you, costs nothing, and contains no calories.

7. ...WITH THE FRUSTRATED AND RESTLESS

If you're one of those grumpy insomniacs who torture themselves and others with gripes and groans, you don't deserve the luxury of sleeping in. Go clean the house, for all I care.

8. TAKE THY SLEEP IN VANITY

Need more convincing? Beauty sleep is not just a myth—sleep also makes you foxy, refreshes your skin, and keeps those unsightly dark circles under control. So don't consider it just sleeping; you're practically working out here.

9. THOU SHALL NOT LOOK AT THE CLOCK

This stressful, possibly evil apparatus can quickly have you counting down the minutes to *Oprah* or worrying how long until lunch. Don't let the ticking second hand score your descent into madness. Remove its batteries or banish it to a bedside drawer, if necessary.

10. KEEP THE SABBATH SLEEPY

Can you even believe there's an official day for sleeping, and it happens every week? Now there's something to believe in. And with the added benefit of your husband, who's there to provide you with all the luxuries you can't be bothered to get up for yourself.

What Does Your Man Do?

Are you ever mildly curious about what your man actually gets up to do once he's left the house, but invariably black out in boredom when he embarks on an explanation? (Something about *buying* and then *selling*.) It's the ultimate unsolved mystery, but the quiz below should give you your first clue.

When he leaves the house, your man wears:

A SUIT
He often complains of a hard day at the _____.

○ **Firm** Good stuff! You've likely landed a lawyer. Watch *The Firm*.

○ **Bank** Congrats! You may be snuggling an investment banker. Go shopping.

○ **Office** Sweet deal! Your man is a nonspecified businessman.

A UNIFORM
What color is his uniform?

- ○ **Blue** Your guy is likely a police officer. Proceed accordingly, minding drug use.
- ○ **Yellow** Lucky! Your man is a firefighter. Get drunk and rent *Backdraft*.
- ○ **Camouflage** Perhaps your man is in the Army. Be sure he fights for whatever side Hollywood's on.
- ○ **Other** Profession unknown. Uniform could be of the stripper novelty variety.

OVERALLS
When returning from work, your man smells like:

- ○ **Paint** Your man may be an artist. Inquire vaguely about "the piece."
- ○ **Gas/oil** Your husband may be a mechanic. Dance around to *Flashdance*.
- ○ **Sweat** Likely construction worker. Enjoy his physique.

OTHER
When his work friends visit, what do they do?

- ○ **"Practice"** Your man may play sports on some kind of team. Note size/shape of ball.
- ○ **"Prepare"** Likely refers to some kind of meeting. You may have a nonspecified businessman of the self-employed form.
- ○ **"Jam"** You might be married to a rock star. Prepare for divorce.
- ○ **"Talk"** You're likely a mob wife. Score!

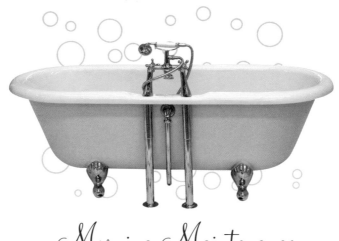

Morning Maintenance

After finally emerging from your cozy hibernation nest, it's time to face another day and meander to the mirror. Yikes! Too many decadent nights have left you looking a little haggard. Good news though: Primping feels as good as it is good for you. Because you can't spend every day at the spa (or can you?), an at-home head-to-toe personal primp regime will quickly get you back to what you're good at: looking at yourself in the mirror all afternoon.

TAKE A BATH If time allows, a morning spent pruning in the bathtub works wonders on the brain and bod. If time doesn't allow, clear your schedule so that it does. Think of all the things you could do at the same time—it's called multitasking and women are good at it. Besides chain-smoking, productive bath tasks include talking on the phone, surfing for porn on the net, dropping breakfast crumbs in the water, and not caring. Products abound: You'll need bath oils and salts; body buffer and butter; boundless bubbles and soapy suds. Add all available bath products to the water indiscriminately and wait for the bubbles to hit the ceiling.

LOCKS YOU'LL LOVE Literally and figuratively dirty? They say wash and repeat, but I say wash and repeat and repeat! Alternate rosewater with lavender, volumizing with smoothing, gentle with extra strength. Next is conditioner; it's like shampoo, only better. Leftovers after the rinse? Keep going. Or did you rinse out the leave-in? Better start all over.

The Decadent Housewife

BODY BASICS Moisturizing is not just for the face. To avoid the confusion of an awe-inspiring range of options, I say go for them all. Exfoliate, mist, oil, polish, lotion, cream, mousse, butter. Yes, it may take a while, but looking this good requires some self-sacrifice. You've cleared your schedule until lunch anyway, and think of the time you're actually saving by not having to work out what each of these products does and which one you need.

FACE FORWARD Like body moisturizing, more is more, but this time the choices are even more breathtaking. Facial scrub, makeup remover (in case, due to circumstances beyond your control, it was not removed last night), cleanser, cleansing oil, toner, moisturizer, age-defying cream (not that you admit or acknowledge wrinkles of any kind), hydrating fluid, face masks, eye contour. Don't argue: Yes, these are all vitally important. Be careful not to incorporate a magnifying mirror—no one's perfect under scrutiny that close.

PUFFY EYES Finally, a use for the green tea bags that clog your coffee cupboard! Just wet and apply. Brew another pot of coffee while you wait.

BLEMISH CONTROL Back when this housewife had a job (I don't want to talk about it), a pesky blemish could easily have me calling in sick to stay home and mope. No time for rationalities; send your husband away for three days and cancel all appointments, so you don't have to leave the house until it's safe to show your face in public again.

Make Ups & Downs

Now no one's suggesting that you ever wake up before your husband to apply a thick mask of war paint. The times when this would impress a man are long gone, and the time where it implies an obsessive-compulsive disorder is right now.

That said, a little touch-up works wonders if you happen to have passed out in your makeup on the porch last night. So whatever you need to do to complete your morning maintenance, choose from the following:

BLUSH Though unfairly bastardized through lesser decades, some well-placed blush will make your unseemly corpse look fit for mingling with the living. Suck in those cheeks like you're blowing kisses to the neighbor and blend color along the bone.

BRONZER Like blush, but bronze.

CONCEALER Don't care how pretty you think you are, I assure you, even the most pompous of supermodels needs this magic product somewhere.

EYE SHADOW/LINER (OPTIONAL) You heard me; this may be the one situation in your day when less is more. Mixed with your red lips, a full smoky eye can be a quick trip to old French whoredom. Unless that's the look you're going for, *ma chérie*.

FOUNDATION Just a dab of this good stuff will instantly have you looking more decadent and less like a swamp monster.

FAKE LASHES If you've come this far, why not go a little further? Fake lashes are the ultimate in decadence, especially if you've got nowhere to go in them. I'm truly impressed!

LIPSTICK Painting your lips blood red is an ancient habit fit for the gods and therefore you. If you don't think you can "pull it off,"

you're not sufficiently decadent. So hit the mall and search high and low for a matte hue that makes you feel like it's lucky to pull *you* off. Nothing like it shows the world you mean business and may bite.

MASCARA Like concealer and lipstick, you desperately need this. Whether you're en route to a soirée or camping in the wilderness (don't ever do this), find the thickest one they sell and layer it on like lead paint. When a stray lash is like a sliver of glass scratching against your cornea, you're ready for your close-up.

NAIL POLISH Repeat after me: I will not leave the house with chipped nail polish. Unless your destination is your manicurist. Remember, false nails of ridiculous lengths are an excellent excuse for avoiding all manual tasks.

POWDER Just when you thought your face couldn't possibly take any more, it's time for powder to complete the set. Now nothing's going anywhere, ever.

Fashion Fundamentals

Fact: Anyone as fabulous as you is cursed to always look good. There's no point in fighting the inevitable; whether dressed to impress in Versace or sealed in plastic wrap at the spa, Decadent Housewives always think they look good—and therefore, they always do.

That said, if you're wearing something older than the millennium but not old enough to be labeled retro and sold back to you at an exuberant price, you might want to take a quick peek at the Decadent Housewife rule book.

A DECADENT HOUSEWIFE FASHION FAUX PAS:
Sharing Your Space

If you've been unwittingly sucked in to sharing your wardrobe space with your husband, all's not lost. This lamentable circumstance is totally reversible and here's how. Firstly, take over a room in the house. The empty nursery, his office, whatever space strikes your fancy. If questioned, stress your feminist right to a dressing room of your own and dismiss your oppressive husband's opinion. Get out the pink paint.

A Decadent Housewife Bonus Tip!

Santa lingerie: Better in theory than application.

A DECADENT HOUSEWIFE GUIDE TO ORGANIZATION:
Keeping Control of Your Wardrobe

There's no point in owning more shoes than
Bloomingdale's if you can't find pairs amid the pile.
Therefore, everything should be organized, OCD-style
(though not necessarily by you). Go even further if
you must: If keeping your shoes in their original
boxes with a photo of said shoes taped to the
outside helps make sense of the madness in
this cruel world, then do it. There's no
judgment here.

A DECADENT HOUSEWIFE FASHION TRUTH:
Hoarding's an Art, Not a Disease

Forget the two-year rule: Keep everything just in case grunge ever
comes back. Do not share your skinny or fat jeans with your
slimmer or fatter friends—you never know when a stomach flu or
all-inclusive vacation may strike. If you've gone and donated all your
options to the Salvation Army, you may end up wearing stretchy
Santa lingerie in May.

THE ULTIMATE DECADENT HOUSEWIFE FASHION RULE:
There Are No Rules

What if you want to fly in the face of fashion authority? Do it. Just
think: Would Madonna follow rules? No, she would sneer at them
and dress like a teenager until the day she dies. So if squeezing into
a trendy asymmetrical top makes you want to do the Vogue, go for
it. Last-minute emergency means you have to fix your Louboutins
with bubble gum? It happens.

Ten Fashion Must-Haves

Remember all that talk about no rules? Disregard. Fashion must-haves include:

FABULOUS DESIGNER PURSE Borrow, rent, or steal as necessary.

FRENCH MAID COSTUME Complete with feather duster, nothing gets you out of cleaning faster.

FRILLY LACE-SKIRTED PANTIES Practical underpants? What for?

JAPANESE KIMONO Unglamorous regular housecoats cannot be compared with the chance to play geisha instead.

LITTLE BLACK DRESS Whether speed-dating or funeral-hopping, baby, you look slender and chic.

MAGIC RED SHOES Ask Dorothy; these have superpowers. Heels should be long and thin enough to kill a man.

PADDED PUSH-UP BRA When they look at least two sizes bigger than they really are, and are barely contained, it's working.

PEARL NECKLACE There's nothing better to trick people into thinking you're a proper lady, when the occasion requires.

PINK EVERYTHING ELSE Pink towels, pink frilly nightdress, pink furry slippers.

RETRO APRONS Oh, there's no dinner, but just look how adorably ironic you are!

The Decadent Housewife

Nothing to Do?

Nonsense. If you find yourself with any free time in the morning, you're not doing it right. Admittedly a properly thorough morning routine involves a lot of steps, so it is understandable if you've missed a couple. So if you find yourself with free time before it can acceptably be called martini hour, check the following:

- ☐ Shampooed, conditioned hair
- ☐ Hair colored, roots touched up as needed
- ☐ Hair blow-dried (also coifed or teased)
- ☐ Hair straightened/curled/sleeked/ defrizzed/gelled as necessary
- ☐ Clay mask to control oil (1 hour)
- ☐ Peel-off mask to add moisture (1 more hour)
- ☐ Face exfolitated
- ☐ Face washed in stimulating half circles
- ☐ Moisturize, moisturize, moisturize (allow to sit 20 minutes)
- ☐ Eyebrows brought under control (may be outsourced)
- ☐ Cucumbers placed on eyes (30 minutes)
- ☐ Eye protector, brightener, and energizer applied
- ☐ Eyelashes curled
- ☐ Lips exfoliated, moisturized, layered with lip balm
- ☐ Body exfoliated, moisturized (you can never have too much moisturizer)
- ☐ Full manicure and pedicure (may be outsourced)
- ☐ Spray perfume into air, walk through

What to Wear?

If your wardrobe has finally attained its walk-in glory, let this chart make the hard decisions for you.

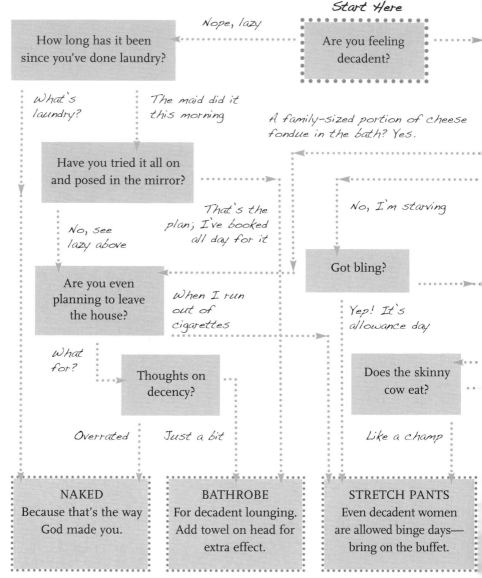

Start Here

Are you feeling decadent?

Nope, lazy

How long has it been since you've done laundry?

What's laundry?

The maid did it this morning

Have you tried it all on and posed in the mirror?

A family-sized portion of cheese fondue in the bath? Yes.

No, I'm starving

No, see lazy above

That's the plan; I've booked all day for it

Got bling?

Are you even planning to leave the house?

When I run out of cigarettes

Yep! It's allowance day

What for?

Thoughts on decency?

Does the skinny cow eat?

Overrated

Just a bit

Like a champ

NAKED
Because that's the way God made you.

BATHROBE
For decadent lounging. Add towel on head for extra effect.

STRETCH PANTS
Even decadent women are allowed binge days— bring on the buffet.

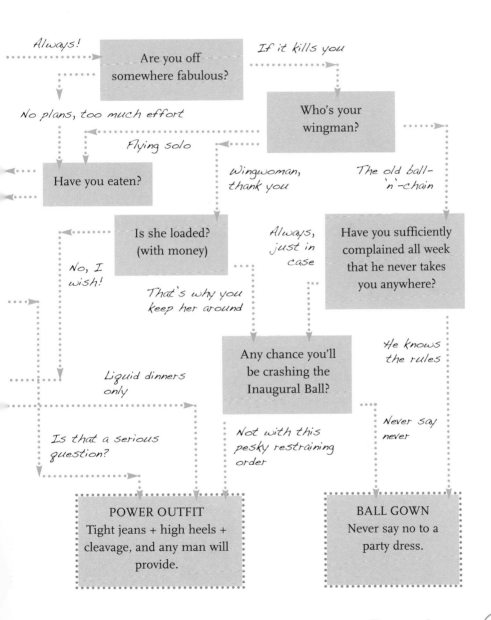

Are you off somewhere fabulous?

Always!

If it kills you

No plans, too much effort

Who's your wingman?

Flying solo

Have you eaten?

Wingwoman, thank you

The old ball-'n'-chain

Is she loaded? (with money)

Always, just in case

Have you sufficiently complained all week that he never takes you anywhere?

No, I wish!

That's why you keep her around

Any chance you'll be crashing the Inaugural Ball?

He knows the rules

Liquid dinners only

Is that a serious question?

Not with this pesky restraining order

Never say never

POWER OUTFIT
Tight jeans + high heels + cleavage, and any man will provide.

BALL GOWN
Never say no to a party dress.

Bawdy Brunches, Lazy Lunches

——

11:30 A.M.–3:00 P.M.

Take a Break

After your morning of leisure and luxury, it's time for your first real task of the day: lunching, decadently. Eating, for some, is merely functional; but for you, it's serious delicious business. Therefore, important decisions like where to go, what to eat, and who will pay (that is, not you) are all part of your job. And unlike dinner, which you may be quite unfairly expected to produce, you have no obligations to fulfill. So there is no reason not to go out and make a boozy afternoon outing of it all with some fabulous friends and/or hunky extramaritals. So spend the morning getting ready, debate which café boasts the best lighting, and mull over entrées for an extra hour. You deserve it!

The Decadent Housewife

What's in Your Fridge?

Beyond the wine rack, your fridge may contain mysteries unknown that are likely to be of the disgusting variety. (If things start to smell funky, it's time to get an investigator in there.) Meanwhile, in case of caterer malfunctions, keep it endlessly stocked with these essentials:

- ○ Shrimp rings and other fancy crustaceans for emergency entertaining
- ○ Pretentious smoked meats
- ○ Cheese in all its glorious forms: brie, blue, cheddar, gouda, roquefort, gorgonzola, fondue
- ○ Chocolate fondue
- ○ Assortment of fruits (of the sexy variety)
- ○ Continuous supply of cheesecake
- ○ Pack of emergency freezer cigarettes
- ○ Cheap champagne for inferior guests
- ○ Overpriced vintage champagne for personal consumption
- ○ White wine, well stocked in case of sudden global shortage
- ○ Hard liquor (for hardcores)
- ○ Lemons, limes, olive garnishes, and other cocktail essentials
- ○ Undeniably decadent products with unidentifiable French names
- ○ Anything that comes with a pastry cup
- ○ Foie gras
- ○ Illegal baby beluga caviar
- ○ Frozen dinners, for husband's emergency sustenance only

Kitchen Gadgets and Doodads

If you require immediate sustenance, and there's no one around to cater to these damn cravings, you might consider what the real housewives call "making something yourself." It's a daunting task, however, and because no one's around to praise your superhuman efforts, I don't recommend it. Still starving and defiant? At least know what's what. You've probably been to the kitchen, so let's start with the basics. The following tools will enable you to whip up something that vaguely resembles a meal.

What the *&$! is this contraption?	Why would you possibly need it?	Where to find it	When you can live without it
	For stabbing food, then delivering said food to your mouth	Placed delicately to the left of the plate, beside its very unnecessary double	You'd rather eat salad with your fingers; you only eat Chinese takeout anyhow
	Cutting food into bite-size pieces; accidentally stabbing your husband in a fit of rage	Stashed slyly with the forks; thrown from a moving car, wiped clean of prints	You're on a liquid diet; he died under mysterious circumstances many years ago
	Transporting soup from the pot to your mouth	Hanging nonchalantly from a well-placed hook	You think "ladling" is "laid" as a verb

The Decadent Housewife

What the *&$! is this contraption?	Why would you possibly need it?	Where to find it	When you can live without it
	Stirring stuff at a rapid pace, something about air...	Who cares, you'll never use it	When they finally develop the electric version to do it for you (that is, now)
	Because you drank all the screw cap bottles at lunch	Keep several in strategic locations around the house so you'll never be without one	You can't
	For layering melted cheese on anything and everything you cook	Wherever you had your last cheese snack	Never! Cheese is always the key ingredient
	Convenient receptacle for refreshment, required to make your sub-par cooking bearable	Bound to be one somewhere near—a red wine stain is a good sign you're getting close	When excessive glass breakages lead to a plastic-only rule
	For cleaning the gunk from sink and other appliances	Leave this manly business to your cleverer husband	If you're clumsier than you are handy and haven't had a tetanus shot

What's Your Dream Career?

Just kidding. But when the chills stop running down your spine, this makes for fun lunchtime banter with your lady friends to make lunch hours fly by. Just don't get any crazy ideas.

1. As the leader in charge, you choose the lunch locale. Where do you choose?

    A) The food court at the local mall.
    B) The lobby café at the swankiest hotel in town.
    C) Anywhere where the menu has high-def pictures.
    D) Your ex-stepbrother's bistro (which may soon mysteriously burn down in a fire).

2. And where do you demand your table, *el Presidente*?

    A) A prime corner table to watch the fashion victims walk by.
    B) Somewhere discreet where you can observe the world from behind your oversized Chanels.
    C) As close as they'll let you to the cake display.
    D) Somewhere near the back door, in case you have to flee an unforeseen raid.

3. Finally, lunchtime. What will you be having?

    A) A chicken Caesar salad with dressing on the side and no chicken.
    B) Prime ribs charged to the nice man in room 412.
    C) Yes, yes, yes. Just bring it all.
    D) A scrumptious lobster bisque, once your food taster has survived the first bite.

The Decadent Housewife

4. You had the oddest dreams last night; what story do you tell during dream-confessional hour?

A) The airport lost your suitcase after a shopping spree in Paris, leading to a full blown fashion tantrum.

B) You were naked in public again—but liked it.

C) A buffet so decadent that you cried when you woke up to nothing.

D) You discovered you can move objects using only your mind.

5. You're obviously not picking up this check, but why?

A) You spent all your money on a new pair of to-die-for Louboutins and now have to walk home.

B) That wasn't part of the deal.

C) You shouldn't be discriminated against because of your addiction.

D) Spoiler alert: Turns out you're the long-lost evil twin of the owner.

How Did You Score?

Mostly As: *Personal Shopper* You're hungry, materialistic, and judgmental: a perfect combination for fashion.

Mostly Bs: *High-class Escort* Just like *Pretty Woman*—without the romantic subplot.

Mostly Cs: *Food Stylist* They pay people to make food look good and then eat it. This could be you.

Mostly Ds: *Soap Opera Villain* Finally, a chance to cash in on your talent for staring down lesser mortals.

Midday Recovery Remedies

Giving up on home cooking already? I suggest a drink. Forget
acceptable social conventions—if your decadence demands a
morning pick-me-up, cheers to you! There's no shame in being
hardcore, so here are a few little something-somethings to start the
day off right or at least get it back on track. Remember to keep the
bar well stocked in case of such emergenices (particularly for
emergency hangover relief, see page 111, "I Need a Bloody Bloody
Mary"). This is really your husband's job, but he may need a gentle
reminder if he underestimates the number of "important" people
you entertain with champagne on a regular basis.

"THE MORNING AFTER"

Not only does this tasty treat take the edge off hazy mornings, it adds an edge to later that night. Remind your hangover who's boss with this twist on the otherwise disgusting and pointless marmalade.

YOU WILL NEED
2 shots (2 fl oz) of gin
1 shot (1 fl oz) of Cointreau
2 tablespoons of fresh lemon juice
1 teaspoon medium-slice orange marmalade

DIRECTIONS
First, feel bad that you even need directions for this. Then pour all ingredients into a cocktail shaker with ice. Shake it like you mean it. Strain into a cocktail glass or coffee mug if you're feeling discreet. Garnish with a thin spiral of orange peel.

"THE MMM-MIMOSA"

You know you're truly decadent when champagne consumption moves from New Year's to birthdays to all days with this addictive dash of deliciousness.

YOU WILL NEED
A glass (6 fl oz) champagne
$^1/_3$ cup (3 fl oz) orange juice

DIRECTIONS
Mix prechilled orange juice and champagne (both live in the fridge, right?). Pour in chilled fancy glass, preferably goblet-sized. Lightweights, add an ice cube.

"AN ESPRESSO IMPRESSO"

Coffee plus alcohol is a decadent way to make your early morning hours happy! This creamy dream gives you your caffeine kick and your booze buzz in one efficient drink. Besides breakfast, the Espresso Impresso works at brunch, during your 4:00 P.M. slump, before dinner, after dessert...OK, anytime really.

YOU DESPERATELY NEED
3 shots of (3 fl oz) vodka
1 shot of (1 fl oz) Kahlua coffee liqueur
dash of ($^1/_4$ fl oz) white crème de cacao
1 shot of (1 fl oz) cold espresso

DIRECTIONS
(And this time you're going to need them.)
Acquire espresso. Pour vodka, Kahlua, crème de cacao, and espresso into a cocktail shaker with ice. Shake it, shake it, shake it. Strain into a chilled cocktail glass. Sip out on balcony, embracing the decadent lifestyle.

A Decadent Bonus Tip!
You're not an alcoholic unless you admit you have a problem. You don't, and you won't.

The Decadent Housewife

Diet Tips and Tricks

Most definitely a decadent housewife, Miss Piggy once said, "Never eat more than you can lift." A good tip for a pig, but if you're battling a swine-sized appetite for brie, you may soon find yourself less decadent and more corpulent. For times like these, there are many sweat-proof, puke-free tricks to keep your muffin-top growth at bay:

A SMALLER PLATE FOR A SMALLER BRAIN If your impressionable brain is dumb enough to fall for this one, then by all means, eat off a saucer.

READ A COOKBOOK If you've ever salivated onto a glossy food magazine or fantasized about the Food Network stars, you know this works like a charm.

BOOT UP AND BOOT OUT Confess your food intake to an anonymous group of judgmental strangers to lose twice as much dignity as those who only annoyed their friends.

DON'T EAT BREAKFAST Or lunch. Or dinner. Frankly, you don't need them, and you'll be fabulously slender by the weekend.

SMOKE MORE AND FASTER Those models are on to something—not only does it suppress your need for nutrients, but it makes you look so cool. Fact.

GIVE UP ALCOHOL That was a trick! Good thing you didn't fall for it.

BET A FRIEND Putting some money on your ability to resist the temptation of cheesecake will inspire you to hold back, while also reminding your frenemies that you always, always win.

STOMACH STAPLING All the fattest, totally has-been celebs are doing it, and therefore, so should you.

Exercise Alternatives for Fitness-phobes

After a breakfast/brunch/lunch feast, you may be plagued with food guilt. But if the mere thought of one more sweaty second on the treadmill makes you want to smash in the bony faces of any fitness freaks who get in your way; if you've already been unfairly removed from your gym for threatening said freaks; or if you'd just rather be fat than move around that much, then there are many ways to retain your decadence and your waistline:

HONE UP WITH HOUSEWORK I would never recommend this, but a very smug website run by a lady sitting on a ball says soaping up your car sucks 330 calories, washing windows wipes off 170 calories and ironing—the most fruitless task of all—burns 150 calories an hour. But on the other hand, why give her the satisfaction?

GET GARDENING Actual gardening is too much like work, so hire a firm, young hunk to do it as you peek through the blinds and admire his handiwork. This still counts as exercise in the form of leisurely strolls around the garden while appreciating the pretty flowers that someone else has grown. It also multitasks as endless afternoon idleness and precious time to work on your tan, all the while masquerading as a viable hobby your husband cannot deny.

KNOCKIN' BOOTS Or so the women's magazines keep telling me. Sleeping only burns 60 calories per hour. Keep that in mind when you go to bed tonight.

SHOP 'TIL YOU DROP (THE WEIGHT)
Forget living longer, boosting your self-esteem, feeling happier, or having more energy and focus on your immediate material wants. Set yourself a basic, realistic goal—I imagine I've been nominated for an Oscar and need something that goes with Leonardo DiCaprio—and walk the mall until you're so frustrated that you faint.

The Decadent Housewife

Exercise Excuses

If whining *I-just-don't-wanna* as you stomp your pumps is garnering judgmental stares from the self-righteous, try out any of these fool-proof excuses:

- ○ Your body's already booked for ovulation this week.
- ○ Germ phobia to bacteria on the machines.
- ○ You're protesting the lack of immediate results—surely lipo is more cost effective?
- ○ Allergic to your personal trainer's cologne.
- ○ You're saving your fast for next year's high-school reunion.
- ○ Religious objection to blasphemous yoga.
- ○ Too distracted by bulging male biceps at the gym.
- ○ Your cleavage looks lackluster in a sports bra.
- ○ Squats disgust you.
- ○ Offended by downward dog position.
- ○ You'd rather be hardcore than have a hard core.
- ○ Still rewarding yourself from last week's workout.

What's Your Fitness Phobia?

If you start the week with good intentions that just keep falling by the wayside, figuring out what keeps getting in the way of exercise can help you overcome the problem. Or at least give you yet another good excuse when explaining to others why you cannot participate in their strenuous Friday afternoon workout.

1. Describe your perfect Saturday night:

    A) Watching *Dynasty* reruns while you snuggle with your man—who doesn't complain even once.

    B) Downing cocktails and mingling with important people.

    C) Turning in for an early night with your man...

    D) An elaborate eight-course dinner at the latest hit restaurant.

2. You have one, admit it: What's your ultimate fitness goal?

    A) Your core mysteriously learns to tone itself.

    B) Making Kate Moss look fat as you stand next to her at a movie premiere.

    C) Getting so flexible you can wrap your legs behind your head.

    D) To eat everything in the world, twice, with no consequences.

3. The doctor says if you don't get 30 minutes of cardio, you'll die. Which of the following isn't a fate worse than death?

    A) A light stroll, followed by a three-hour catnap—sleeping burns calories and therefore, must be counted as exercise.

    B) Power walking through the fashion district in a pair of four-inch Manolos.

    C) An evening spent working hubby through the *Kama Sutra*.

    D) Enthusiastic mashing of a bowl of potatoes.

The Decadent Housewife

4. When was the last time you broke a sweat?

A) Presenting your social science project at school.
B) You don't sweat; you glisten.
C) Last night (I know you know what I mean).
D) Last week when you had to wrestle your husband for the last piece of Brie.

5. Your gym snob friend insists you take a fitness class. Which do you choose?

A) Meditation. Breathing's not too bad...you guess...
B) Kickboxing. It's trendy, it's social, and if you ever have to deal with anyone who gets in your way, you'll know how.
C) Salsa dancing. Not just a dance, it's practically foreplay.
D) Cooking. Maybe if you stand the whole time, and whisk like you really mean it, it'll somehow count.

How Did You Score?

Mostly As: Laziness is impeding your path to physical fitness. At least you get your beauty sleep. Consider the express surgery route instead.

Mostly Bs: Your fabulousness naturally steers you away from public sweating. There's nothing fab about flab though, so just fast like the stars do.

Mostly Cs: Luckily, your favorite pastime burns calories anyway. And he could do with the workout, too.

Mostly Ds: What would decadence be without indulgence? Though it might be time to start exercising your restraint at least.

The Lost Art of Idleness

3:00–5:30 P.M.

Household Gadgets and Contraptions

Whether or not the maid's arrived this week, or if you've secretly hired a muscle-bound helper to wash your windows for you, it's important to be able to identify the basic cleaning contraptions. They're lurking in some back room closet in your home, and while hopefully you'll never have to actually use them, recognizing them is key. Should your husband ever ask, not knowing an iron from a food processor could have disastrous lifestyle consequences.

Mystery apparatus	Official use by real housewives	Why you don't need it	Your Decadent alternative
	Forcefully sucking dirt into a localized pile	Loud noises upset your fragile condition	Turned on for sound effects while you don earplugs and do a sudoku
	Brutally manual version of above contraption	Because you're pretending to use the vacuum instead	Riding in circles around a full moon
	Washing dishes and prolonging your manicure	Too busy getting said manicure	The god of all kitchen appliances: the dishwasher

The Decadent Housewife

Mystery apparatus	Official use by real housewives	Why you don't need it	Your Decadent alternative
	Redistributing particles into the air	Crippling dust allergy	Tickly accessory for foreplay
	Disinfecting killer germs from all available surfaces	You're keeping the bacteria as pets	Ensuring you're the blondest babe that ever was
	Removing unsightly kinks from your husband's old clothes	Husband no longer trusts you with his remaining shirts	Removing unsightly husbands from your kink for new clothes
	Vigorously scrubbing floors	Fresh out of elbow grease	Third step of elaborate pedicure routine
	Vigorously scrubbing toilets	Pure disgust	Assign him bathroom duty today and forever for bedroom favors

The Superficial Clean

Your husband, unenlightened as he is, may consider housework to be your "job." This is a good time to explain to him about your rights as an empowered woman and that jobs are for suckers, which is why you don't have one.

That said, there's nothing decadent about loitering in your own mess all day, so keeping up a general level of cleanliness between maid services is essential. It's called the Superficial Clean, and you're about to become an expert.

KITCHEN   Begin in the kitchen (that's the room with the food); if this should turn out to be your only successful task of the day, you can consider it a sufficient achievement. First, anything you're not willing to eat should be tossed, as should any dish too dirty for the dishwasher. There's no reason you should have used a pot, but if for any reason you were so brave/foolish, it is your husband's legal obligation to complete said task in light of all your commendable cooking efforts. It's either that or buy you a new one. Push all remaining countertop items into the sink. Cover sink with a dish towel.

VACUUMING   This literally sucks. Think about pushing around a great big heavy dirt machine that roars, and then think again about investing in wood flooring. If you insist on an area rug, try this: lift rug, shake off dust and accumulated mess, push said mess into localized pile, cover pile with rug. Done.

A Decadent Bonus Tip!
Invest in an air freshener. If you didn't clean today, then why does it smell so damn good in here?

BATHROOM If the kitchen's food factor wasn't bad enough, I double dare you to check out your bathroom. Filthy bathroom habits plague both sexes and your bathroom is likely home to all kinds of tiny mystery creatures. Luckily, many large and possibly evil corporations have invented all kinds of chemical sprays that are sure to squash bacteria and brain cells alike. Spray said chemicals liberally after your morning bath, take a great big whiff for the road, and use the powder room for the rest of the afternoon.

LAUNDRY A much-dreaded but sadly necessary task. Unless you just buy new clothes (more power to you) or you can somehow make it through the day without spilling a vodka cranberry on your pajama bottoms (see Stain Removal Rescue, page 78), laundry must be done or else you'll end up wearing ball gowns and old Halloween costumes. There's a simple, nonracist trick to this: the white and nonwhite system. Divide accordingly, add a pile of soap proportional to how dirty you've been, and press the button.

REAL CLEAN A cruel irony: The Superficial Clean only works, sort of, when accompanied by a regular Real Clean. This does not mean, however, that you should attempt this by yourself. Arrange for professional help to restore order to your headquarters... preferably an apron-clad hunk who can help tackle those hard-to-reach areas.

Afternoon Appointments

An idle afternoon isn't complete without an enjoyable but imperative appointment (but never two, there's no need to rush or swamp your day). Enjoy your health-care benefits (your husband pays for it anyway), and pamper your mind and body with regular afternoon dates with a variety of professionals and their various levels of personal necessity. Plus, with all the necessary preresearch, making yourself presentable and a relaxing stroll uptown, this could take all day.

BIKINI WAXER It's good pain; you know you love it. Well, you're going to put up with it anyway.

DENTIST Because flossing is disgusting, and you'll pay whatever it costs.

DOCTOR This might take several appointments with different doctors before you find the one suited for your needs—preferably a hunky one of the TV variety.

HAIRSTYLIST Change your hair color and style at least once a month, like a spy.

GYNECOLOGIST Though many women apparently hate this, enjoy the attention!

MANICURIST Because every time you chip a nail, a fairy dies. Or something like that...

MASSEUSE You have a stressful life, and the morning was tough going, you deserve a brief time-out.

NUTRITIONIST In case you think dipping cheese blocks into melted chocolate might be healthy, it's not. Pay someone to tell it to you straight.

PEDICURIST Could be done simultaneously with the above, but that seems like a waste of a perfectly good excuse for a double pampering session. Why cram it all into one?

PERSONAL TRAINER So you can disregard the nutritionist and make the ultimate fondue feast again tonight.

PLASTIC SURGEON Don't cry: A little Botox pick-me-up will fix those frown lines. And if that doesn't work, a little eye job will stop the tears altogether.

PSYCHIC Because how else will you know what to do for the rest of the day?

THERAPIST If a whole uninterrupted hour of talking about yourself sounds like a reason to fake manic highs, this is the comfy couch for you.

Where to Go Today?

Now that the house is "clean," it's time to decide what to do. So don't be plagued with indecision; follow the dang chart:

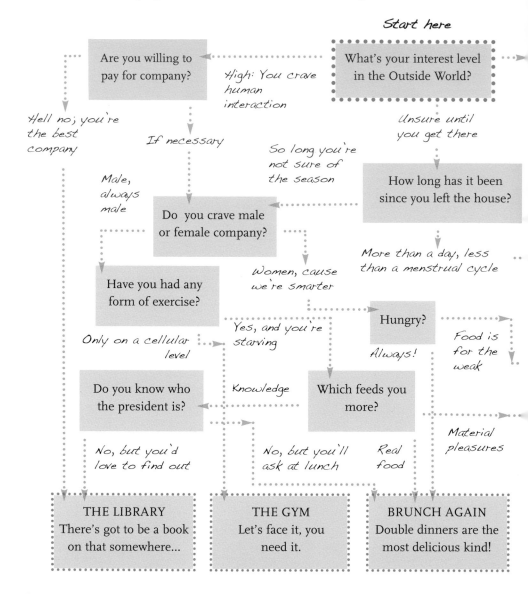

Start here

What's your interest level in the Outside World?

Are you willing to pay for company?

High: You crave human interaction

Hell no; you're the best company

If necessary

Unsure until you get there

How long has it been since you left the house?

Male, always male

So long you're not sure of the season

Do you crave male or female company?

More than a day, less than a menstrual cycle

Have you had any form of exercise?

Women, cause we're smarter

Hungry?

Only on a cellular level

Yes, and you're starving

Always!

Food is for the weak

Do you know who the president is?

Knowledge

Which feeds you more?

No, but you'd love to find out

No, but you'll ask at lunch

Real food

Material pleasures

THE LIBRARY
There's got to be a book on that somewhere...

THE GYM
Let's face it, you need it.

BRUNCH AGAIN
Double dinners are the most delicious kind!

The Decadent Housewife

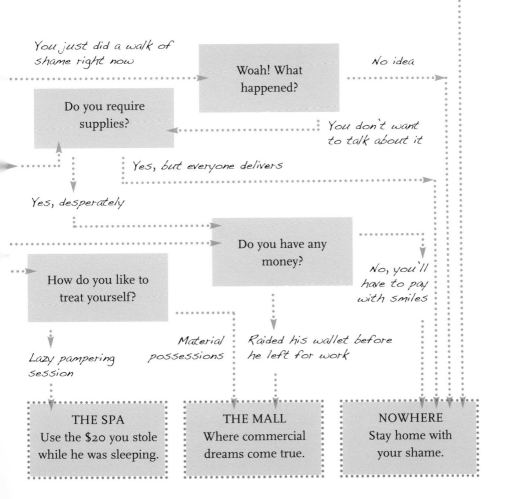

None: You hate everyone

You just did a walk of
shame right now

Woah! What
happened?

No idea

Do you require
supplies?

You don't want
to talk about it

Yes, but everyone delivers

Yes, desperately

Do you have any
money?

No, you'll
have to pay
with smiles

How do you like to
treat yourself?

Material
possessions

Raided his wallet before
he left for work

Lazy pampering
session

THE SPA
Use the $20 you stole
while he was sleeping.

THE MALL
Where commercial
dreams come true.

NOWHERE
Stay home with
your shame.

Recommended Classes and Courses

Don't worry. Unlike the 8:30 P.M. homework hell that you remember, these classes are fun and unfailable (though not unkicked-outable). And if you happen to have a crush on the teacher, no one calls the authorities. Take that, high school!

ALCOHOLICS ANONYMOUS If you take a friend and get drunk first, this can be a lot more fun than it sounds.

ART CLASSES Whether you have a gift for still-life or pine to draw portraits, your crappy art is a critique-free zone guaranteed to kill the afternoon. Plus your art doubles as free gifts to people who are too polite to complain.

BALLET (OR TAP, OR BALLROOM) A time killer that also eats calories, dance classes don't have to be the social torture you remember. Especially if you're the thinnest girl in the class.

BOOK CLUB If you're bored already, consider forming your own. A champagne-fueled critique of this week's *Enquirer* counts completely.

COMPUTER CLASSES Just kidding; you're not a robot.

COOKING I know what you're thinking. But at least you can say you tried.

CRAFT WORKSHOP/KNITTING CIRCLE/QUILTING BEE Sitting around with a group of old gals whose stitches are straighter than their sexual preferences may feel as if you're trapped in a sap fest, but rest assured, those old bats are dirtier than you are.

FLOWER ARRANGING A little-known gem of a course,

featuring pretty flowers and smiles. Plus you get to keep the bouquet and pretend you bought it, because you're sad that your husband never buys you flowers anymore.

FRENCH (OR SPANISH, OR ITALIAN) If your French is limited to *voulez vous coucher avec moi?* followed by a drunken wink, it's time to dust off the old translation dictionary. And this time, forget verb congregation and stick to the dirty words. *Ya de merde!*

MAKEUP If these classes don't exist in your hood, throwing your own makeup party where you "whore up" the first girl who passes out is a perfectly acceptable alternative.

PHOTOGRAPHY Pervs rejoice! Developing your own pics is your final revenge on judgmental pharmacy workers.

PIANO/VIOLIN/FLUTE Everyone knows musical inclination is a gift that makes you smarter, but be warned: Learning to play an instrument is both hard and boring. Take each lesson once and quit in a huff.

POLE/BELLY DANCING Yoga doesn't get you in the mood? Here's a slutty girl's excuse to get sluttier.

PSYCHIC READINGS Fine-tune your witch powers with some old-school aura reading. I see a very frightened man in your future.

SELF-DEFENSE What's better than self-empowerment? Learning to kick your husband's ass.

SELF-HELP SEMINARS There are a billion self-help books with varying levels of legitimacy and each one has a mantra-singing, book-plugging meeting of crazies to match.

What Kind of Faux Artist Are You?

If you're looking to choose a suitable afternoon pursuit (don't worry, it's not as exhausting as it sounds), first figure out which area of the arts you excel in—or would have excelled if anyone had taken the least interest when you were in your prime.

1. Describe your childhood art that your parents stupidly didn't acknowledge.

    A) Endless pencil sketches of Leonardo DiCaprio.
    B) Cassette tapes of you rocking out on the pots and pans.
    C) A homemade dress of wrapping paper and scotch tape.
    D) Lying facedown on the floor until somebody bought you an ice cream.

2. Why were you so cruelly removed from art school?

    A) Because society won't yet recognize your genius (just like Van Gogh).
    B) Because you just don't believe in the treble clef.
    C) Because your collages made of fashion magazines weren't winning you the respect you deserved.
    D) Because they said romantically pursuing the nude model isn't art.

3. Presented with a pile of buttons and an artistic challenge, what do you do?

    A) Glue them randomly to the walls in an exercise of postmodern chaos.
    B) String them on dental floss for a funky wind-chime effect.
    C) Decoupage them on an antique vase and then go flower shopping.
    D) Throw them out of the window, shouting "You're free!"

The Decadent Housewife

4. Good news! You're throwing an art party, and your husband can't stop you. Whom will you invite?

A) The less-talented members of your painting class who make you feel better about yourself.

B) A questionable Rolling Stones cover band who lets you play the triangle if you answer to "groupie."

C) Your knitting circle of merry widows.

D) A slightly oddball group you met on the Internet, on the condition that no one speaks.

5. Your shrink asks you to present your state of mind via art. And your answer is...?

A) A delicately painted tracing of your hand giving the middle finger.

B) You belt out a "Let It Be" reprise, replacing "It" with "Me."

C) You crochet yourself into a cocoon and cry it out.

D) You stop taking showers and insist on sleeping in a cardboard box.

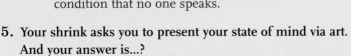

How Did You Score?

Mostly As: *Viva la Visual Artist* Your genius lives in visual art. Start enthusiastically applying paint to random surfaces. Talent's so overrated anyhow.

Mostly Bs: *New Wave Musician* You are clearly destined for musical superstar status. Now if you could only carry a tune...

Mostly Cs: *Craftaholic* You love to do it yourself, admit it.

Mostly Ds: *Persistent Performance Artist* Your whole life is art! Don't even think of toning it down.

TASK ELONGATION:

A Not-So-Brief Introduction

Like nondecadent people, your life is full of tasks. There are things to drop off and pick up, things that need buying or selling, things to be fixed or quietly disposed of. For most, these minor irritations must be unnaturally squashed into lunch breaks or after work—resulting in major irritations. They can't possibly do them right in that amount of time.

A Decadent Housewife knows that if something's worth doing at all, it's worth taking your sweet time over it. Whether returning a book (you'd best make a scene) or acquiring a birthday card (this can take weeks), a truly Decadent Housewife can stretch them out, do them right, sprinkle them liberally with diversions and distractions, and enjoy the rightful justification they provide to slack off for all day tomorrow. Now let's look at an example.

A LESSON IN TASK ELONGATION:
A Case Scenario

The situation: You have been asked by your husband to purchase a bottle of wine for tonight's dinner party with his business colleagues. An equal fan of wine and businessmen, you have happily obliged.

✗ THE "SIMPLE" SOLUTION:

Grab a bottle of red on your way home from the grocery store.

✓ THE "DECADENT" SOLUTION:

STEP 1 First, call the hostess and invite her to lunch. Immediately call your hubby with hard evidence of your demonstrated interest and effort in his boring mystery profession.

STEP 2 Inquire over appetizers about the evening's menu in order to match wine selection appropriately. Test a few varieties with lunch.

STEP 3 Leisurely stroll to the bookstore, purchase book on wine pairings. Read book in park while suntanning. Take detailed notes.

STEP 4 Walk to the local wine store and ask to speak to the manager. Emphasize the importance of you and the evening's event. Flirt with the manager to obtain samples of top choices. Record the selections in chart form, and request more time to think. Instead use the time and afternoon buzz to try on dresses at a department store.

STEP 5 Meander home, a pour glass of wine. Three glasses later, remember you were supposed to buy the wine. Call your girlfriends for second opinions. Google "wine home delivery," but get distracted by personality quizzes. Learn what your name means.

STEP 6 Interrupt hubby's business meeting. Explain frantically how fast your day filled up. Remind him how busy you are, and how cute you look in new dresses. Suggest he grab a bottle on his way home.

Cocktail Hour

5:30–7:30 P.M.

Happy Hour

Great news! It's officially time to celebrate the end of the workday (this is the first hour you acceptably pour yourself a drink, you swear). And doesn't Happy Hour seem so much happier when you haven't had to go to work all day? So kick the neighbor out of your house (because hubby's home soon) and get your after-work friends in. It's time to have a bit of fun.

A Decadent Point to Ponder

As the "work" day draws to a close, it's time to ponder your achievements of the day. Although self-reflection (and its bitch cousin, self-control) are the sworn enemies of decadence, a little contemplation on the day can help you justify your existence and fondly look forward to taking it easy tomorrow. So pour yourself a stiff something and ask, "Have I been sufficiently decadent today?"

Have I...

- ○ Admired my superior posing abilities in the mirror?
- ○ Seriously entertained the possibility of modeling?
- ○ Decided instead to stay home with the kids?
- ○ Remembered kids are exhausting, and taken a pill for that?
- ○ Eaten a crumbly snack on his side of the bed?
- ○ Had five complete minutes of gentle exercise?
- ○ Spent 45 complete minutes with a masseuse?
- ○ Painted my nails, disliked the color, and repainted?
- ○ Bathed morning, noon, and evening with different-smelling soaps?
- ○ Screened my phone calls all day so people know I'm important?
- ○ Called one frienemy at work to boast of my lax lifestyle?
- ○ Watched a complete episode of *Sex and the City*?
- ○ Nagged my husband about something minute?
- ○ Bothered him at work to apologize and blame the hormones?
- ○ Fallen asleep in one strange and unnatural location?
- ○ Drunk one bottle of wine like doctors recommend?

Do You Understand?

You know how it goes: Your husband charges through the door like a thundercloud. He's had such a hard day, he sighs. While you try your best to feign interest, he interrupts and mutters viciously, "Like you'd understand." He said what now? You heard me. Now handle it:

1. **How do you respond?**

   A) Politely inform him that sarcasm is the lowest form of wit and that's why you're the brains of the operation.
   B) Blow up on him. He doesn't understand how many coats of nail polish chipped before you got looking this good.
   C) Let the comment slide and make yourself another martini.
   D) Kiss him on the neck and ask him if he'd explain it to you.

2. **How long is this going to take? Now he's going on and on about his awful boss.**

   A) Suggest that he save the drama for his mama and be a real man.
   B) Speaking of real men, inquire about his boss. How old is that silver fox, anyhow?
   C) Tell him not to worry. You ordered surf and turf on his Visa, and it's already on its way.
   D) Nod methodically, but with a really suggestive look in your eye.

3. **Same problem as above, but it just keeps on going! What should you think about as he talks?**

   A) The lovely ladies of daytime television. It's lucky you have them to fill your brain with thoughts of meaning.
   B) How relieved you are that you don't have to go to work. It's so spirit crushing.
   C) How good your skin looks in the whites of his eyes.
   D) Any of the above; anything but what he's actually saying.

The Decadent Housewife

4. **Yikes! He's got this weird look on his face, and it's getting scarily emotional. How to deal with it?**

A) Ask him why his afternoon smile is somehow upside down.

B) Interrupt the sob-fest to point out how his wrinkles pop out when he cries.

C) Brag that you have no wrinkles at all, thank God.

D) Pull his head into your cleavage and pretend that this never happened.

5. **It seems the girly complaints are finally dying down. Now's a good time to:**

A) Tell him how much today's *Oprah* spoke to you and begin acting it out.

B) Remind him how funny it is that you haven't held a job since waiting tables in college.

C) Mention how the afternoon kitchen fire was completely not your fault, and you're therefore, not paying for it.

D) Surprise him with good news! You're throwing him a party...right now.

How Did You Score?

Mostly As, B's, or C's: WRONG! Any more of this and you may induce a full on man-trum. Obviously such sessions are a bore and a waste of your time, but domestic bliss (and continued access to the credit card) demands careful man management.

Mostly Ds: Correct, my Pet, great work! You know to flatter, flirt, and show your boobs as needed to keep the peace.

What Did You Do Today?

Oh no, the dreaded question. Hubby's home and, statistically, he's already not happy. A bad response will not lead to the carefree fun-filled evenings favored by Decadent Housewives the world over.

THE WRONG ANSWER? The truth. Your husband is guaranteed not to recognize or appreciate all your accomplishments of the day (your immaculate appearance, for example, is an enviable achievement in itself). He may instead be angered by your purchases and dismissive of your understanding of the word "necessity." He may object to the company you've been keeping and suspicious of the man concealed in the hallway closet. The truth, you see, may be simply too decadent for him to bear.

ANOTHER WRONG ANSWER? "Nothing." A resentment-inducing response as such could quickly encourage suggestions that your lifestyle is unfair, lacks meaning, or is not worth funding.

THE RIGHT ANSWER is vague and cryptic, since a Decadent Housewife must always keep the mystery going. Say you went "out," perhaps you "needed some things," or maybe you're "getting your thoughts together." But whatever you say, you'd better get the house—and your story—in order.

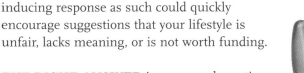

Perfecting Your Alibi

○ **DO** change out of your towel and into something absolutely
   show-stopping.

○ **DON'T** mention why you're dressed for success. (As far as he
   knows, you were volunteering with lonely orphans.)

○ **DO** replace the take-out menus you've been reading with the
   New York Times.

○ **DON'T** mention the expensive new negligee you charged to
   his Visa. Once he's seen it on you, it won't occur to him to
   argue about the cost.

○ **DO** invent a project (screenplay, interpretive dance,
   mathematical formula) that has been consuming your time
   and energy.

○ **DO** have a momentary "breakthrough" and exit the room when
   he probes for details.

○ **DON'T** answer the phone during the day so you seem busy.

○ **DO** leave frantic messages on his machine about your stress
   level, time constraints, and inability to produce dinner
   tonight. Or tomorrow.

○ **DON'T** forget to turn the channel from the Food Network to
   CNN before he gets home.

Party Themes

As if you needed a reason, but when decadence turns to excess, you may benefit from an explanation for your sponsor or probation officer. Luckily, any of these will do just fine.

YOUR UNBIRTHDAY Since no one can make you get any older on a day that is not your birthday, why not throw a very merry un-birthday party to celebrate your eternal youth? Bloody Marys all around. This is a particularly good excuse, because it can be applied to any party any day of the year bar one.

SUPERBOWL Husband be damned; you're laying claim to the flat screen for an all-day marathon of bad rom-coms. There'll be no chili, no beer, and no balls.

SUMMER SOLSTICE Time to call the corners, witches! The longest day of the year deserves a party, and it's an excellent way to get through that many daylight hours. It's also a good time to strip naked and put curses on people you used to hate from high school.

BACK-TO-SCHOOL DAY Bonus points—now you won't have to see children during the day anymore, and you can relax safe in the knowledge that you don't have to wake up early for math class.

HALLOWEEN Quite simply the best religious holiday ever invented, Halloween is your free pass for sin and debauchery, and you can do it all while dressed as a bunny. Why else do you have that closet of costumes?

LABOR DAY Every day is Labor Day because you don't believe in labor, so make a toast to poetic justice.

NO-BABY SHOWER Another year's gone by without insemination? Pour yourself a drink, because you can.

The Decadent Housewife

Party Games for Party Girls

Now I know what you're thinking: Party games are what losers who don't go to parties imagine parties are like. That's often true; there's no fun in wearing a sticker reading Paris Hilton on your forehead while raving about how you love going downtown. That said, a well-lubricated game can entertain and humiliate your guests for years to come. Remind people whose party it is with these forced festivities.

"The Rules"

HOW IT GOES An oldie but a goodie—each guest makes one annoying random rule. Rule breakers drink more and faster.
SUBTLE SUGGESTIONS No name calling; no laughing at your own jokes; no drinking without saying "Cheers!" first.
WHY IT WORKS The more rules you break, the harder it is to follow the rules. Or remember the rules. Wait, what rules?

"The Psychiatrist"

HOW IT'S DONE One player (the least clever or most intoxicated) is chosen to be the "psychiatrist." They leave the room while the group decides on a shared neurosis. When the psychiatrist returns, they ask questions to diagnose as hilarity ensues.
WHOM TO INVITE Pervs who play doctor, depressants who need cheering up, your therapist.
WHEN TO SKIP IT Guest of honor has OCD; you're actually hearing strange voices.

"The No Game"

YOU WILL NEED A house full of open-minded strangers; a box of leis.
HOW TO PLAY Each guest is given a lei. They mingle accordingly, but if another person convinces you to say "No," they score your lei. Most leis is the winner; the prize is, uh, leis.
WHY YOU'LL WIN You haven't said "No" to anything yet!

The Party Décor Decoy

If your husband resists the party, it's too late. The guests are invited and on their way, the bar has been stocked to overflowing, and you've been slaving over party bites and hors d'oeuvres all day. Sort of.

Besides the guests (whom you invite is important in order to get a well-rounded variety to keep the party interesting—always make sure you include one gossiper, a glass breaker, and someone who always tells sexually inappropriate stories), your party setup is the key to successful mingling, which in turn is the key to a party that people talk about for weeks to come. Poor planning can lead to pileups in the kitchen as you cry in the bathroom, so for the sake of your sanity and non-waterproof mascara, plan ahead.

CENTRALLY LOCATED STEREO A well-placed stereo system can lead to either a sweet jam fest or someone's unabashed picks of slow rock, so grant music access sparingly by hiding the remote.

HIDE YOUR TV Besides protecting your flat screen from the storyteller's/glass breaker's clumsy second act, moving your television also prevents anyone from uttering "What? You haven't seen *Willy Wonka and the Chocolate Factory*?" as they turn off the music and reach for the DVD.

BAN THE CHILDREN There are definitely and definitively no children allowed at your party, without exception. Anyone who dares to bring children will not be invited back. Should they appear, one of the offending parents will be banished for the duration of the party to be put on "kids room" duty. That should teach them.

THE BEDROOM'S A NO-GO ZONE Recall all the times you've done it for kicks in the hostess's waterbed, and then invest in an electric fence.

REARRANGE YOUR FURNITURE Move things aside and away as necessary, like a grade-school dance. You'll thank me when the Whitney Houston ballad starts and the red wine begins to flow beyond the boundaries of the glasses.

AND NOW COVER THE FURNITURE Think you're too fancy for plastic throws? When the storyteller recounts their Vegas trip and the glass breaker falls backward over the sofa arm, you'll be whistling a different tune. You have been warned.

DIM THE LIGHTS Now no need to go for full blown romantic mood lighting and whip out the candelabra, but if your soiree seems more like a science lab, it's time for your husband to man up and install a dimmer switch. No one wants to see other people's pores under fluorescent lights.

A Decadent Bonus Tip!

Karaoke is a sloppy mess that no self-respecting housewife would enjoy. Save your rendition of "Total Eclipse of the Heart"—and your dignity—for the shower.

Cocktails and Mocktails

A steady supply of alcohol means your guests won't notice any of the finer details of the party that you skimped on or couldn't bother with (see Easy Hors d'Oeuvres, page 76). These tasty delights will have your party guests letting loose long before polite social customs allow. (I was just kidding on those mocktails, by the way; let drivers drink tap water, I say.)

"THE PINKEST LADY"

A girly drink if there ever was one, three of these power-feminist gems will lower the tone of any gathering faster than you can say "unladylike."

YOU WILL NEED
1 shot gin
$^1/_3$ cup (3 fl oz) milk
2 shots whipped cream
grenadine for color

SLIGHTLY-LESS-THAN-SIMPLE DIRECTIONS
Add all above ingredients in a shaker with ice. Shake and strain into champagne/similarly celebratory glass. Garnish with cherry.

The Decadent Housewife

"THE SCREAMING ORGASM"

Doubling as a drink or a shooter, this creamy concoction is just as enjoyable as orgasms seem on TV.

YOU WILL NEED
1 shot (1 fl oz) Bailey's
1 shot (1 fl oz) Amaretto
2 tablespoons (1 fl oz) cream
1 shot (1 fl oz) Kahlúa

SUPER-SIMPLE DIRECTIONS
Mix ingredients above, serve with hearty dose of sexual innuendo.

"AN EVEN LONGER ISLAND ICED TEA"

Lightweights beware: This blackout juice contains a much higher alcohol concentration than its many less-fun alternatives. So when you wake up in a taxi and nothing looks like your suburb anymore, this postion is probably why.

YOU WILL NEED
1 shot (1 fl oz) vodka
1 shot (1 fl oz) gin
1 shot (1 fl oz) tequila
1 shot (1 fl oz) rum
a splash of cola, for color

DANGEROUSLY SIMPLE DIRECTIONS
Mix all the alcohol in the world in a tall glass over ice.
Consume recklessly and without regard.

Easy Hors d'Oeuvres

As your guests become sufficiently liquored up (see page 74), their expectations of you, as well as their standards of eating, will decrease. Suddenly, anything that comes with a dip and is arranged nicely on plate will suffice. They may even commend you on the hours you must have slaved in the kitchen to produce such delights. Try these fabulous finger food tricks to make less seem like more.

CHEESE AND CRACKERS Might not sound like much but it's all how you sell it. Don't say crackers, say crostini. Don't say cheese, say the particular kind of cheese in your best French accent. Invest in impressive gruyères and gorgonzolas. (Cream cheese, however, is eternally banned from your party.)

CREATIVE PARTY MIX Pretzels? Commonplace. Peanuts? Seedy. Pretzels plus peanuts? Deliciously bold. Add wasabi beans and you're ethnic. Present them on the silver tray of a kid with a bow tie. Done.

MINI SOUP BOWLS Here's your instant trendy appetizer. Serve any canned soup in a trendy little cup or microsized square bowls and your snobby guests are sure to find postmodern satisfaction. Rename your creation: Anything green is Elegant

A Decadent Bonus Tip!

Can't work the stove? Restaurants deliver teeny-tiny foods, too, and they're inevitably better than anything you'll ever make. Just saying.

Herbed Purée, everything else is Sherried Spicy Consommé. This can also double as an appetizer for pretentious guests at the dinner party you haven't told your husband you're having later.

OLIVES Whether swimming in your martini or baked atop your pizza, nature's hors d'oeuvres are the easiest way to take your party from poor to posh without turning on the stove. (FYI: It's that turn-y knob on the right. Turn it off again before your flesh singes.)

PHYLLO CUPS A long-held staple in every pretentious party circle. You can buy these little morsels in any grocery store. You could stir croutons with barbeque sauce, and as long as it's served in a phyllo cup and introduced as Mediterranean, it will be a success.

SHRIMP Important people love shrimp. Ask any man in a suit if he would like a shrimp, and he will say, "Yes please, sweetheart." No fuss or botheration required: Defrost precooked shrimp, arrange on china dish, sprinkle with something, and dip it into something else. Delish!

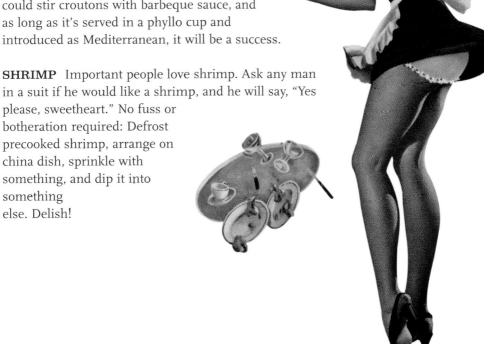

Stain Removal Rescue

Besides the questionably deliberate tripping into the buffet table (true story), nothing kills your party mood like an embarrassing tell-all stain. Ordinarily you might be tempted to just throw your outfit out and buy a new one, but sometimes you need to make it through the rest of the evening fully clothed. Therefore, stain removal is one domestic skill that all Decadent Housewives do actually need in order to look their best while keeping incriminating evidence at bay. What evidence? Exactly.

What's that on your dress?	How'd that happen?	Traditional remedy	Decadent remedy
	Six morning cups of this, and just see how shaky you'd be	Flush with white vinegar to remove the brown hue	Turn pajamas inside out and pour another cup
	Your pretentious green tea drinking habit is being punished by the Party Gods	Flush with lemon juice to remove color, then water if you've snuck in sugar	You've clearly still not left the house yet— just change the outfit
	The sneaky little devils keep escaping your grasp to hide between the couch cushions	Wash with dish washing liquid for grease, dab with white vinegar for color	Eat chocolate in bar form from now on

What's that on your dress?	How'd that happen?	Traditional remedy	Decadent remedy
	You tried to baste yourself for slow cooking	Wash with dishwashing liquid, dry flat	Bump into someone eating greasy finger food and place all blame at their door
	Enthusiastic toasts have expensive long-term consequences	Use denatured alcohol (oh, the irony!), dab with white vinegar, rinse with cool water	Wear dark, spill-proof colors in the future
	Same as above, but during first course	Dab with cool water, dry flat	No need at all; that's why you cleverly chose white in the first place
	Momentary curiosity got the better of you	Spray stain with hairspray	Pin flower over stain. So cute and seasonal it was clearly an intentional addition
	Sometimes you bite	Soak in cold, salted water overnight	A well-placed bandage and corresponding tale to garner sympathy

Hospitality without Hostility

—

7:30–11:30 P.M.

Decadent Dinners

Despite all its glory, cocktail hour is just that—an hour. Well in your case, it's been two, but that's not the point. The real point (if you'd only stop distracting me) is that if your guests don't eat, they may die. The last thing you need is legal responsibility for whatever shenanigans are about to go down, so just for good measure, serve somebody *something*.

Anatomy of an Invitation

Make your dinner party official with invitations. Then if your husband resists your plans, it's too late; you mailed the invites weeks ago. And how cute does it look all pink? Exactly.

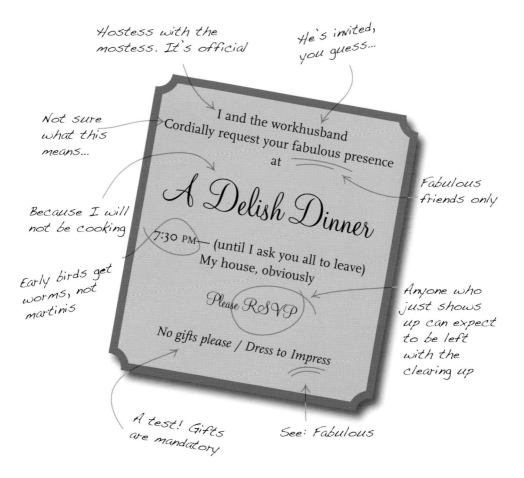

Hostess with the mostess. It's official

He's invited, you guess...

Not sure what this means...

Because I will not be cooking

Early birds get worms, not martinis

I and the workhusband
Cordially request your fabulous presence
at

A Delish Dinner

7:30 PM — (until I ask you all to leave)
My house, obviously

Please RSVP

No gifts please / Dress to Impress

Fabulous friends only

Anyone who just shows up can expect to be left with the clearing up

A test! Gifts are mandatory

See: Fabulous

The Guest List

Contrary to what better housewives may tell you, the foundation of a decadent dinner party lies not in the dinner, but in the party. Whom you invite—and why you invite them—is as important as the caterer showing up. Here's a who's who of necessary party dwellers.

THE HUSBAND He can come, if he must, provided he funds the whole thing and keeps all comments and complaints to a minimum. But you needn't sit beside him.

THE HOT NEIGHBOR Sit beside him instead. Besides reminding your husband what he's aiming for, a muscled ball of eye candy will ensure you're sufficiently relaxed and titillated.

THE HOT NEIGHBOR'S LESS-HOT DATE Extending the invite to his girlfriend with the "lovely personality" can only make you look better. (Bonus points if her awkward self doubles as a glass breaker.) Unfortunately, there's no particular way to enforce whom he dates and contrarily, a superhot date can make you the homely sidekick.

THE PROFESSOR Not a real professor, per se, but a guest who reads the paper can be an invaluable aid in solving any budding political disputes (Where *did* the Soviet Union go?) quickly, before such conversations take over your gathering.

The Decadent Housewife

THE GOSSIPER That's not to say a little malicious gossip isn't welcome, so you'll need a shameless attention addict who can't help but spill secrets (as long as it's not your secrets). She likely has some of the sexually inappropriate variety, but if not, leave that for your next guest.

THE LUSH Make a point of inviting someone with an inability to handle alcohol. It's a little enabler action on your part, and no matter what happens, you can always deflect attention by recalling when the Lush put her shoes on the wrong feet.

THE GIFT GIVER Because you can't say "No" to Dom Pérignon.

THE SCAPEGOAT A well-placed scapegoat can solve many party problems: Want to get dinner rolling? Your scapegoat may go into diabetic shock. Ready to send everyone home? The scapegoat's afraid of the dark. Pick someone meek who won't object to the blame being laid at their door for obscure incidents they had nothing to do with.

THE PUSHOVER A pushover is a pal whom you can ignore throughout dinner but insists on/can be bullied into staying to clean up while you go fix your manicure. You need her terribly.

Seating Plan

This is as important as the guest list itself, and not just because of the footsies. If you have been forced to invite people you don't like, it is very important to make sure that you are not going to have to sit anywhere near them.

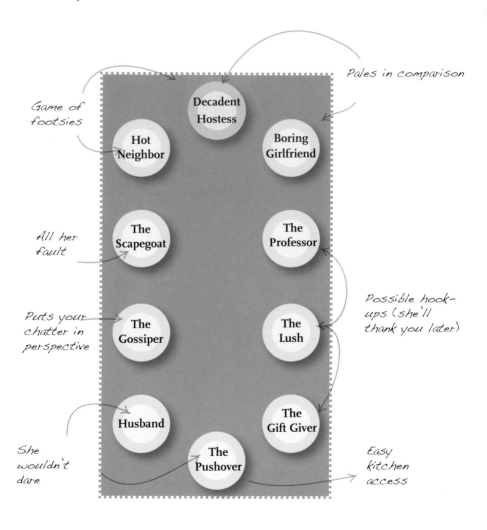

Pales in comparison

Game of footsies

Decadent Hostess

Hot Neighbor

Boring Girlfriend

The Scapegoat

The Professor

All her fault

The Gossiper

The Lush

Possible hook-ups (she'll thank you later)

Puts your chatter in perspective

Husband

The Gift Giver

She wouldn't dare

The Pushover

Easy kitchen access

The Formal Place Setting

A dinner party is much like a Cocktail Party (see previous chapter), but without the part where you ditch your table. In this case, the table's very necessary, in case your guests resort to eating over the sink. Even more important is what's on the table, so pay attention.

Save dessert or cutlery, you'll be sorry later

"Rehydration" (or liquor backup location)

Red wine: the inevitable progression from white

White wine: the old broad's looser-upper

Salad = last = classy

Napkin, on lap, gross food, in napkin

Start here, obviously!

Stabbing knife (just in case)

For soup slurping

Dinner Party Themes

Having a theme might sound like unnecessary effort, but it can actually make the evening a whole lot easier. With a clear theme in place, the organization can be swiftly delegated to anyone in your immediate vicinity and with minimal instructions. It's all much like the Party Themes (see page 70), but then food arrives at your door. Preferably the back door, with the packaging swiftly disposed of so you can pass it off as your own. You make it all look so easy.

Inspiration	On the menu	What you need	Dress code
	Deep-fried tidbits and doodads; things that are both sweet and sour	Chopsticks and a little help from your friends at your local take-out	Full kimonos for women; samurai armor for men
	Champagne, olives, and caviar	Even you should be able to handle that on your own	Red carpet, ballgowns
	Red wine, crusty bread, pasta in sauces, more wine	Local pizza parlor will do just fine	Any designer with an Italian-sounding name

The Decadent Housewife

Inspiration	On the menu	What you need	Dress code
	Vodka martinis, lemon twists	Nonjudgmental dinner guests	Platforms and sequins
	Tapas, enchiladas, margaritas	Only tequila can ensure the success of the evening	Beads, sombreros, peasant skirts
	Murder and mayhem	The butler, a French maid, a rich elderly man	Long gloves, a look of innocence, and a gun in your garter belt
	The Hot Man from your guest list	His cell-phone number and a group code word	New lingerie that hubby bought (though he doesn't know it yet)
	Fried chicken, fried cornbread, and fried peanut butter sandwiches	The greasy staff of a fast food chain	Cowboy hat, hair gel, lowered party standards

How's Your Dinner Etiquette?

1. **It's all meet and greet, all the time. How do you introduce a priest to an old broad?**

   A) "Father, I'd like you to meet Mrs. Nightingale. Mrs. Nightingale, this is a priest from a church I never go to."

   B) "Uh, this is, uh, P-p-priest—it was an accident, I swear to God, you can't prove anything."

   C) "Priest, meet Delores. You two cats are similarly judgmental."

   D) "Hey Ma'am, a priest! Get a load of that V-card."

2. **It's time to sit down for dinner, but how's your table posture?**

   A) You could balance a phone book on your head if necessary—you've practiced all afternoon.

   B) Your frozen limbs keep knocking over the salt shaker.

   C) You sit cross-legged and accidentally show off your underwear.

   D) The chair's so damn uncomfortable that you take your plate to the sofa.

3. **Mid-soup, your phone blasts a Destiny's Child ringtone. What next?**

   A) Turn it off immediately and apologize that Beyoncé didn't RSVP.

   B) Check who it is, make up a cousin who's deathly ill, and invite everyone to next week's wake.

   C) Explain that you bought this phone because you're an independent woman and refuse to apologize.

   D) Answer it (loudly): "Hello darling! No, *nothing*. I'm so bored I could die."

The Decadent Housewife

4. You can't possibly eat another bite until dessert! How do you signal the end of main course?

A) Push all your food in a localized pile and fervently set your silverware parallel across it.

B) Dump all your leftovers into your napkin and hide it behind a curtain.

C) Hold your plate up until the help takes it away.

D) Lick the gravy clean and smash the dish to the floor.

5. And what's the last line you mutter as you usher out the last guest?

A) "You're so welcome for being invited."

B) "Your husband looked superhot tonight."

C) "Just for the record, my party has once again surpassed your party."

D) "Let's just never speak of this again."

How Did You Score?

Mostly As: *Mildly Mannered* You could take definitely Miss Manners in a girl fight.

Mostly Bs: Awk-*ward!* You try, but your presence gives everyone the creeps.

Mostly Cs: *Politely Passive Aggressive* Way to show those other hostesses who rules.

Mostly Ds: *Completely Inappropriate* You'd best stay home alone and make your own etiquette.

The Party Commandments

You strive to be a smug and gracious hostess—where generosity is emphasized as rage is suppressed. It's an illogical inverse to your day-to-day conduct, but with a little practice hostessing with the mostessing can be all yours—provided you and your guests know the rules. It's as simple as obeying the Party Gods and, luckily for you, they sent me their commandments if I gave them my soul.

1. THOU SHALL NOT ACCEPT EARLY ARRIVALS
If you find yourself franticly extinguishing kitchen fires and hiding sex toys in the final minutes before your party, the last thing you need is an awkward presence offering to toss your salad. Unless invited, anyone who arrives even fifteen minutes early should not be admitted.

2. THOU SHALL NOT EMBRACE LATECOMERS
The opposite, of course, is equally unbecoming. Stumbling into a trickling scene and demanding where the party's at is a good reason to tell them to stay at the club tonight.

3. EMPTY-HANDED IS THE DEVIL'S WORK
Bringing nothing—not a loaf of bread or a bottle of Bordeaux—is a sure sign that the guest in question should never be invited back.

4. HONOR YOUR HOSTESS AND YOUR HOST
This commandment goes both ways—because you've refrained from smashing their china and trying on a hostess's wedding gown, so should they.

5. THOU SHALL EAT AND BE MERRY...
Hand in hand with no complaining, a gracious guest shall eat what's presented and feign joy while doing it. That's right, *joy*: No one wants to hear about gas prices, fibroids, or how the football season is going. It's your job to make sure that rule is followed.

6. ...BUT NOT TOO MERRY
We all dig a sweet buzz, but if you're closing one eye to get the doubles under control, if you've already thrown up once tonight, or if standing on a table seems like it'll just prove your awesomeness, it's time to call it a night and leave your husband with the task of sending people home and cleaning up.

7. A GUEST SHALL NOT TONGUE KISS ANOTHER GUEST'S WIFE
Unless you're throwing that special kind of party, tongues always belong in the tongue-owner's mouth.

8. COMPLAINERS WILL BE THROWN TO THE LIONS
Do not, under any circumstances, accept complaints or suggested improvements to the following: food choice and preparation; home location or decoration; hostesses' choice of ensemble, professional choices, or fitness routine; other people's marriages; the government; or the weather.

9. THIEVES DESERVE ETERNAL DAMNATION
While a subtle peek into your medicine cabinet is forgivable (Valium? Get out!), any guest popping the bottle into her purse with a dozen rolls and a roll of fancy toilet paper is on a fast track to party purgatory. Don't even think of forgiving those with sticky fingers.

10. GUESTS SHALL SPREAD FORTH THE PARTY LOVE
Every time your guest takes another egg roll, he shall be reminded that the party rule of three dictates he now owes the universe a bigger and more delicious egg roll. Point out that bad party karma is not a fun curse, and a reciprocal dinner invite should follow.

Late Nights, Early Mornings

11:30 P.M.—

In the Bedroom

There's no sexy secret here: The bedroom is where and how a Decadent Housewife gets and wields her greatest power. As such, dictating occasion (mornings? get real) and location (bedroom or otherwise), frequency (lunar cycle), and style (who knows what you get up to) is all part of exercising and maintaining your decadence. So just do it, or maybe don't, and here's how.

Phone Sex Etiquette Checklist

Credit card bills keeping your husband late at the office? Keep fears of secretaries at bay with some well-timed phone calls. This is best attempted only if he has his own office. (If he doesn't, he clearly needs the late nights to work his way up that ladder.) Follow these simple rules to avoid any phone faux pas.

- ○ **DON'T** secretly phone a girlfriend on three-way calling for joke fodder for later.
- ○ **DO** still engage if you're not in the mood—faking is permissible in phone sex.
- ○ **DON'T** accidentally dial your dad's office.
- ○ **DO** gulp your wine and tell him he tastes so good.
- ○ **DON'T** drink until you vomit and tell him he makes you gag.
- ○ **DO** make a cheese plate beforehand to keep you entertained, and your energy levels up.
- ○ **DON'T** inadvertently replace his name with "Brie."
- ○ **DO** enthusiastically repeat the words "big," "hard," and "deep."
- ○ **DON'T** mention the phrases "average size," "mild satisfaction," or "I can't feel anything."
- ○ **DO** run the blender in the background for effect.
- ○ **DON'T** actually incorporate the blender.

What's Your Love Style?

1. You obviously demand attention to get you in the mood, but what?

    A) To be stroked like a cat for the whole afternoon.
    B) A large pizza that you refuse to share.
    C) Dancing in a cage at your local strip club.
    D) Waited on for days like a sheik.

2. In your most intimate love fantasies, which romantic gesture rules?

    A) He ties you to the bed where your only job is to receive pleasure.
    B) He carries your limp body from the couch to the bedroom.
    C) He invites the neighbor over for some gentle male muscle touching.
    D) He's hired a maid and a cook for a year.

3. He wants to what? No way! But why?

    A) He was selfish with his credit card last year, and you haven't forgotten.
    B) You already pretended to work out once today.
    C) You just watched that in a porn movie and know you can top it.
    D) Unwilling to mess up expensive asymmetrical haircut.

The Decadent Housewife

4. Showtime. What's your best performance technique?

A) Begging for it, but by "it," you mean a nullified prenup.
B) Subtle moaning as you dream of your fantasy man.
C) Repeatedly dropping the f-bomb in verb, noun, and adjective form.
D) Reenacted scene from *Basic Instinct,* minus the ice pick.

5. Ah, you've done it again. How do you take your postcoital bliss?

A) Alone in the bathroom with your personal massager.
B) Another uninterrupted month of platonic hangout.
C) A planned succession of questionable extramarital excursions.
D) In soft lighting and 400-thread-count Egyptian cotton.

How Did You Score?

Mostly As: *Too Selfish* Your entitlement is commendable, but try to give a little back.

Mostly Bs: *Too Lazy* Your presence is your present, but at least move around a bit.

Mostly Cs: *Too Slutty* Don't think you're that slutty? Then why are you dressed like a bunny?

Mostly Ds: *Devilishly Decadent* Great work! You're a decadent inspiration to us all.

Location, Location, Location

Bored of the bedroom? It's time to venture out. Now your bed's just for food and feminist biographies, like nature intended.

Bedroom alternative	How it's done	Possible perks	But watch out for
	Frantic efficiency, on the counter, over before the pans boil over	Retro aprons; proximity to the refrigerator	Steak knives; preheated ovens; food contamination
	Just like the kitchen, but during the spin cycle	Oh, *you know*	Spilled bleach; mixing your lights and darks
	Multitasking suds with studs	Removable showerheads; it's effortlessly steamy; you're already clean	The bathtub: That doesn't work, so even don't try
	Against the glass with the blinds slightly ajar	Letting your neighbors know who's still got it	Drafty panes; Peeping Toms

The Decadent Housewife

Bedroom alternative	How it's done	Possible perks	But watch out for
	Perched on the desk, after hours	Having officially gone to work today	Misplaced staples; unpaid overtime; developing a work ethic
	Comfortably and lazily as Letterman delivers his monologue	Casually watching 9½ Weeks in your peripheral vision	Inconspicuous channel changing to the football game
	With superior dexterity and balancing skills	You're already done by the time you reach the bedroom	Carpet burn; right angles; a shoddy banister
	On the floor, preferably on a bearskin rug in front of a roaring fire	Room to stretch; toasty temperatures; supporting the fur trade	Flammable underpants; slivers; mice

Who's Your Fantasy Man?

Of course, your husband is pretty close, but there's always room for improvement (in other people), and fantasies don't count as cheating.

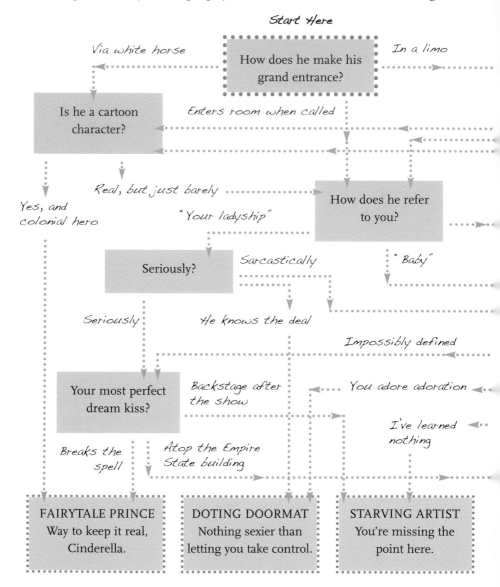

Start Here

How does he make his grand entrance?

Via white horse — **Is he a cartoon character?**

In a limo

Enters room when called

How does he refer to you?

Yes, and colonial hero

Real, but just barely

"Your ladyship" — **Seriously?**

Sarcastically

"Baby"

Seriously — **Your most perfect dream kiss?**

He knows the deal

Impossibly defined

Backstage after the show

You adore adoration

I've learned nothing

Breaks the spell

Atop the Empire State building

FAIRYTALE PRINCE
Way to keep it real, Cinderella.

DOTING DOORMAT
Nothing sexier than letting you take control.

STARVING ARTIST
You're missing the point here.

The Decadent Housewife

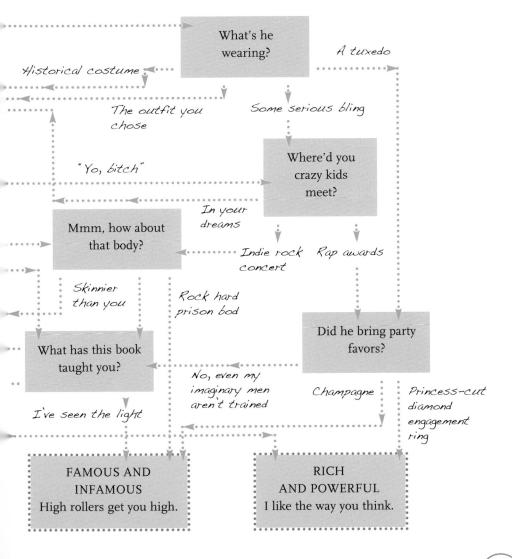

What's he wearing?

A tuxedo

Historical costume

The outfit you chose

Some serious bling

"Yo, bitch"

Where'd you crazy kids meet?

Mmm, how about that body?

In your dreams

Indie rock concert   *Rap awards*

Skinnier than you

Rock hard prison bod

Did he bring party favors?

What has this book taught you?

No, even my imaginary men aren't trained

Champagne

Princess-cut diamond engagement ring

I've seen the light

FAMOUS AND INFAMOUS
High rollers get you high.

RICH AND POWERFUL
I like the way you think.

Dress Ups to Get Down

For the especially decadent, and a little bit deviant, a little role-play action is a great way to do things you otherwise never would and then deny it later. Any of these creatively ensembled scenarios are guaranteed to get you out of—and into—some serious trouble. They are also useful as a means of distraction from any acts of deviant decadence that your husband may not immediately comprehend the importance or necessity of in the maintenance of your lifestyle.

Object of inspiration	You will need	In the script	When to get real
	A leather outfit, a stern disposition, a baton	"Anything you say can and will be used against you"	The real cops have arrived
	An apple, a kilt, an unacceptable grade	"Please, Mr. Husband, I'll do anything"	You're fourteen; he's someone else's husband
	A lab coat, a stethoscope, basic medical terminology	"The doctor will see you now"	He seems to actually be showing symptoms of E. coli

Object of inspiration	You will need	In the script	When to get real
	A velvet outfit, a festive spirit, a lax humiliation factor	"But sometimes it's nice to be naughty"	It's summer
	Waist-length hair, a long-lost twin, a nonjudgmental attitude	"You're my rebel hero"	There are fifty thousand of them at this brutal convention
	A bunny outfit, a basket of pastel eggs, an impressive high-jump score	"Hop! Hop! Hop!"	You're just crazy enough to boil yourself
	A feather duster, a crinoline petticoat, a butchered French accent	*"Oui oui, monsieur, j'aime votre argent.*	He's got the wrong idea and actually expects you to clean something.
	Something painful and leather, stilettos, repressed rage	"Shut up! SHUT THE *&#$ UP!"	Your house isn't soundproofed and your neighbors are starting to complain.

Ailments to Fake

Sometimes you're just not feeling it. Lots of times, actually. But in the heat of the moment, a poorly placed excuse (a pimple, it's raining, you'd rather watch *Wheel of Fortune*) can push a frustrated husband to the brink of sexual madness. So forget the overused headache, and use one of these gems instead. If he starts looking suspicious or unwilling to accept any of these as a valid excuse, a dramatic fainting episode and insistence on ordering an ambulance works like a charm.

- Nausea
- Pregnancy
- Menstrual cramps
- Leg cramps
- Herpes breakout
- Constipation
- Mononucleosis
- Hysteria
- Amnesia
- Coitophobia
- Melancholy
- Feminism
- Phallophobia
- Disillusionment
- Temporary homosexuality
- Heterophobia
- Papercut
- Shin splints
- Hallucinations
- Caffeine withdrawal
- Germaphobia
- Aversion to sweating
- Psychosis
- Asexuality

The Decadent Housewife

A Night Out Gone Bad

Though it is (usually) enjoyable to entertain in your own home (and preferable again to just show up at someone else's), there will be late night occasions when a Decadent Housewife finds herself in other, less entertaining, places. Here are a few less-than-fabulous places where she should call a cab and go home.

DANCE CLUB If you're over 22 years old or 120 pounds, there are no unshameful times to be had at a dance club. Your cheeky dinner buzz can easily get ugly with a few tequila shots, and before you know it, you're grinding with your gal pal to Bon Jovi. When anyone asks your major, takes a picture of you for his website, or calls you a MILF, it's time to go home.

SPEED DATING If 25 men in 25 minutes feels less porno and more man-of-your-dreams, and your single friends are forcing you to join them, maybe you should try speed dating. But be warned: like college, it all blurs into one vague evening and you'll inevitably find yourself on...

A BLIND DATE Though the reality show was awesome, the chances you'll end up on a date with a hunky bachelor are much smaller than the chances your date is a sexual predator, and they'll have to identify your body via dental records. Also where's your husband?

BOWLING This is neither fun nor fabulous. Decadent Housewives do not bowl, play bingo, or participate in any sport in mini form. If you can't perform the entire evening in your Louboutins, don't perform it at all.

A Decadent Housewife Bonus Tip

Remember: Whoever finishes the first glass of wine the quickest, successfully dodges the role of designated driver for the night.

Mastering Your Sleep-a-Thon

Rumors say sleep is cumulative, so in case you ever find yourself on a 72-hour crime spree, you'd best start storing up your shut-eye hours now. Most scientists say grown-ups need around seven hours, but they're likely grumpy losers consumed with jealousy of your newborn-style sleep schedule. So forget the "facts," I say, because as usual, more is more. Here's how it's done.

FINALIZE THE GUEST LIST You and your husband may attend. With all romping already taken care of, now tell him firmly and well in advance that your sleep sessions are the foundation of your decadence and as such, no more funny business is on tonight's menu. You need your beauty sleep, and a little more, so touchers will be promptly relocated to the couch.

CULTIVATE A STATE OF EXHAUSTION Of course, I don't buy it, but someone in a lab said too much sleep conversely makes you more tired. Shows what those lab coats know, because that's exactly

A Decadent Housewife Bonus Tip!
The alphabet game, done decadently:
don't count sheep, count ex-boyfriends.
A is for Aaron, B is for Brett...

what you're aiming for. When you can get around 10 hours and still nap before dinner, you're doing it right!

RETREAT TO YOUR ULTIMATE SLEEP CAVE Please refer to various interior decorating shows on this one, but the gist goes as follows: comfy plush bed, blue paint not orange, thick curtains better suited for a bordello.

NO CLOCKS ALLOWED The ultimate trick to satisfying slumber. Knowing the time will just remind your brain that the outside world exists.

TRAINING YOUR BRAIN Passing out is easy, as is slipping on a puddle and knocking yourself unconscious. However falling asleep gracefully and without chemical intervention can be hard work. The trick, used on small children and well-trained dogs, is a schedule. Do the same thing every night: eat a feast, drink a bottle of red in a bubble bath, and read suggestive novels until your subconscious can't take it anymore.

STILL CAN'T DOZE? Insomnia is the opposite of decadence, so handle it before it handles you. If it's 4:00 A.M. and you're still staring at your ceiling, remember, they make pills for that. Thanks, science!

Hangover Cure

No, it's not "Moderation the Night Before," and frankly, no one likes your attitude. So if you've been shooting tequila until five but need to be in court by nine, you know that getting yourself together is a fine blend of hippy herb drinks and pretending you didn't just vomit in the car. Remedies vary in time and effectiveness, but try any and all of the following.

THE NIGHT BEFORE If you are a clever alcoholic, not that I've ever met one of these robots, two big glasses of regular tapwater before you pass out may transform your morning from crunky to funky. Of course, if you're fit to make such a plan, you might not be as inebriated as you think you are, and it's therefore, perhaps not the work of the water after all. Deductive reasoning, folks.

THE MORNING OF Hardcores, take note. Set your alarm an hour early (I know, but bear with me) and quickly consume a quart of hydration, two extra-strength painkillers, and an oversized bagel. Put a pillow over your head and go back to bed at once. Water plus chemicals plus carbs plus nap will have the judge fooled in no time.

SLEEP IT OFF It never feels like it at the time, but a whole day moaning and watching made-for-TV movies on a women's network is really not as bad as it sounds. Factor in no diet restrictions and a license to be irrational all day, and you've got a pretty nice afternoon in your future. Enjoy it.

PILL POPPING Good news! Whether you've got a headache from hell or a churning stomach, someone makes something for that. Stick to the legal ones.

GREASY BREAKFAST Some women swear on a greasy morning-after breakfast. Jury's out on whether it works, per se, but you sure look awesome in last night's clothes and oversized sunglasses.

COFFEE, COFFEE, COFFEE Technically coffee dehydrates you and is therefore, the opposite of what you want. But if skipping it altogether makes your flulike symptoms feel more like the plague, by all means, double up.

DRINK MORE But if the java's just not cutting it, it may be time to mix yourself a mood elevator. See below for a healthy(ish) drink to follow. No one can judge you in your current sensitive state.

"I NEED A BLOODY BLOODY MARY"

If it comes to this, do remember that antioxidants to your organs are like a shot of vodka to you, and invite them to the party, too.

YOU WILL NEED
$^1/_2$ cup tomato juice
juice of one lemon
dash of Worcestershire sauce
celery salt
ground pepper
hot pepper sauce to taste
2 shots (1 fl oz) vodka (mandatory)

DIRECTIONS
(for your husband, of course)
Over ice, blend ingredients in tall glass.
Garnish with celery stalk and lemon wedge.
Enjoy in excess; learn nothing.

Late Nights, Early Mornings

In Conclusion...

So that's it, ladies, another decadent day done! Remember all we've accomplished together: woken up, primped, ate, drank, ate and drank, performed a single errand, primped again, acquired a dinner, thrown a party and got your party on. All while looking and feeling fabulous, and that's no easy task.

Some might disagree. They may say your decadence isn't valid or useful, that you are "a disgrace to your gender," or "everything that's wrong with the world today." Don't listen to those grumps, and try to turn the other cheek as Oprah once famously said we should. Those grouches probably missed their morning sleep-a-thon, dragged their uncomfortably attired zombie bod into traffic or even the dreaded and disgusting public transit, only to spend the whole long day in an office smaller than a prison cell. Their anger and resentment is understandable, and the two hours you spent trying to bake a cake to cheer them up isn't helping.

But others are on your side: me, your lunching lady friends, the producers of daytime television. They know that decadence is a lost art and that those brave enough to cultivate it are to be rewarded with health and happiness, low-blood pressure and wrinkle-free faces, endless pleasure, and fruitless self-expression. So shamelessly enjoy your day, your house, and your free time, and don't let anyone—your husband, your mother, the police, society at large— suck the pleasure from being decadent.

Now it's time to say goodnight. Your progress has been swell and your decadence is imminent: Today's been lush and lavish, well used and well enjoyed. But even decadent housewives earn some much-needed shut-eye, so rest up—we'll be doing it all again tomorrow.

The Decadent Housewife